SING WE NOW OF
CHRISTMAS

Arranged by Dan Goeller: Created by Mark Edwards & Dan Goeller

11
TIMELESS CAROLS
FOR TODAY'S STUDENT
CHOIR

PRODUCTS AVAILABLE:

Choral Book 0-6330-9132-4
Listening Cassette 0-6330-9134-0
Listening CD 0-6330-9133-2
Accompaniment CD (Split track) 0-6330-9135-9
Cassette Promo Pak 0-6330-9141-3
CD Promo Pak 0-6330-9140-5
Orchestration 0-6330-9144-8

GENEVOX

SING WE NOW OF
CHRISTMAS

presents anew some old material that your student singers may not have heard, but are sure to enjoy. There are nine settings of time-honored Christmas carols, plus a surprise or two. Some of the carols were not "sacred," per se, in their original contexts. Dan Goeller has tastefully synthesized those with other musical material that "baptizes" the original songs. The results are meaningful expressions of joy and celebration at Christ's birth.

The arrangements are fresh and well crafted for teenage voices. They are conceived chorally, the vocal parts are linear, and accompaniments serve the singing voices. Do not allow the interesting and sometimes intricate rhythms (and rhythm sections, if used) to compete with the singing voices. This would defeat the purpose of this collection. Both SATB and SAB versions are included to make this accessible to more students.

Program Notes are located in the back of the collection, so your singers and congregation can understand more about the background of the selections. These notes may be included in a written program or worship folder, or members of the student choir may read them as introductions to the selections.

Since I was on the creative team for this project, the student choir at First Baptist Church, Nashville, Tennessee, had the first opportunity to sing these exciting, new arrangements. We enjoyed them from day one. The music was accessible, but not readily; it was challenging, but well worth our efforts.

Blessings on your work with teenagers! We hope this collection provides a rich expression and experience for your students as they "Sing…**Now** of Christmas!"

— Mark Edwards

CONTENTS

SATB / SAB

Bring a Torch, Jeanette, Isabella! with Angels We Have Heard on High ... 7 / 103

Good Christian Men, Rejoice with Joy to the World! The Lord Is Come ... 45 / 119

Lovely Child, Holy Child ... 78 / 133

O Come, All Ye Faithful ... 86 / 137

O Come, O Come, Emmanuel ... 17 / 108

Pat-a-Pan ... 24 / 111

Sing We Now of Christmas with Antiphonal Noel ... 69 / 129

Still, Still, Still ... 34 / 116

The World's Desire ... 56 / NA

What Can I Give Him? ... 97 / NA

What Child Is This ... 63 / 125

INSTRUMENTATION

Bring a Torch, Jeanette, Isabella! with Angels We Have Heard on High

Rhythm, Violin I, Violin II, Viola, Cello, String Bass

Good Christian Men, Rejoice with Joy to the World! The Lord Is Come

Fiddle/Whistle/Pipes, Rhythm

Lovely Child, Holy Child

Rhythm, Violin I, Violin II, Viola, Cello

O Come, All Ye Faithful

Rhythm, Violin I, Violin II, Viola, Cello, String Bass

O Come, O Come, Emmanuel

Synth Whistle, Synth Dulcimer, Synth Boy's Choir, Synth Pizzicato Strings, Rhythm, Violin I, Violin II, Viola, Cello, String Bass

Pat-a-Pan

Rhythm, Violin I, Violin II, Viola, Cello, String Bass, Whistle

Sing We Now of Christmas with Antiphonal Noel

Rhythm, Violin I, Violin II, Viola, Cello, String Bass

Still, Still, Still

Rhythm, Violin I, Violin II, Viola, Cello

The World's Desire

A cappella

What Can I Give Him?

Rhythm

What Child Is This

Rhythm, Violin I, Violin II, Viola, Cello, String Bass, Whistle

Bring a Torch, Jeanette, Isabella!

with Angels We Have Heard on High

Traditional Provençal Carol
Arranged by Dan Goeller

Has - ten now,___ good folk of the vil - lage,

Has - ten now,___ the Christ child to praise! Re -

joice!___

O Come, O Come, Emmanuel

Traditional*
Arranged by Dan Goeller

*Latin Hymn tr. John Mason Neale & Henry Sloan Coffin. Music Plainsong; adapt. Thomas Helmore.

come to thee, O Is - ra - el!

Pat-a-Pan

Words and Music by
DAN and HEIDI GOELLER
Adapted from a Burgundian Carol

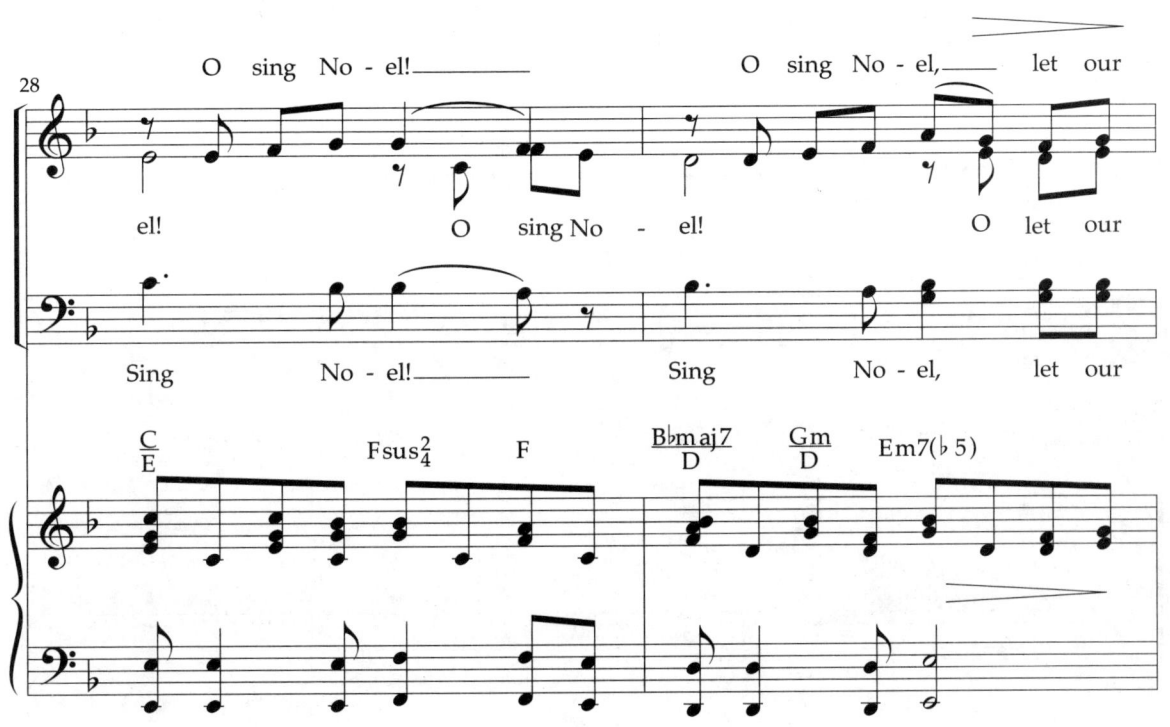

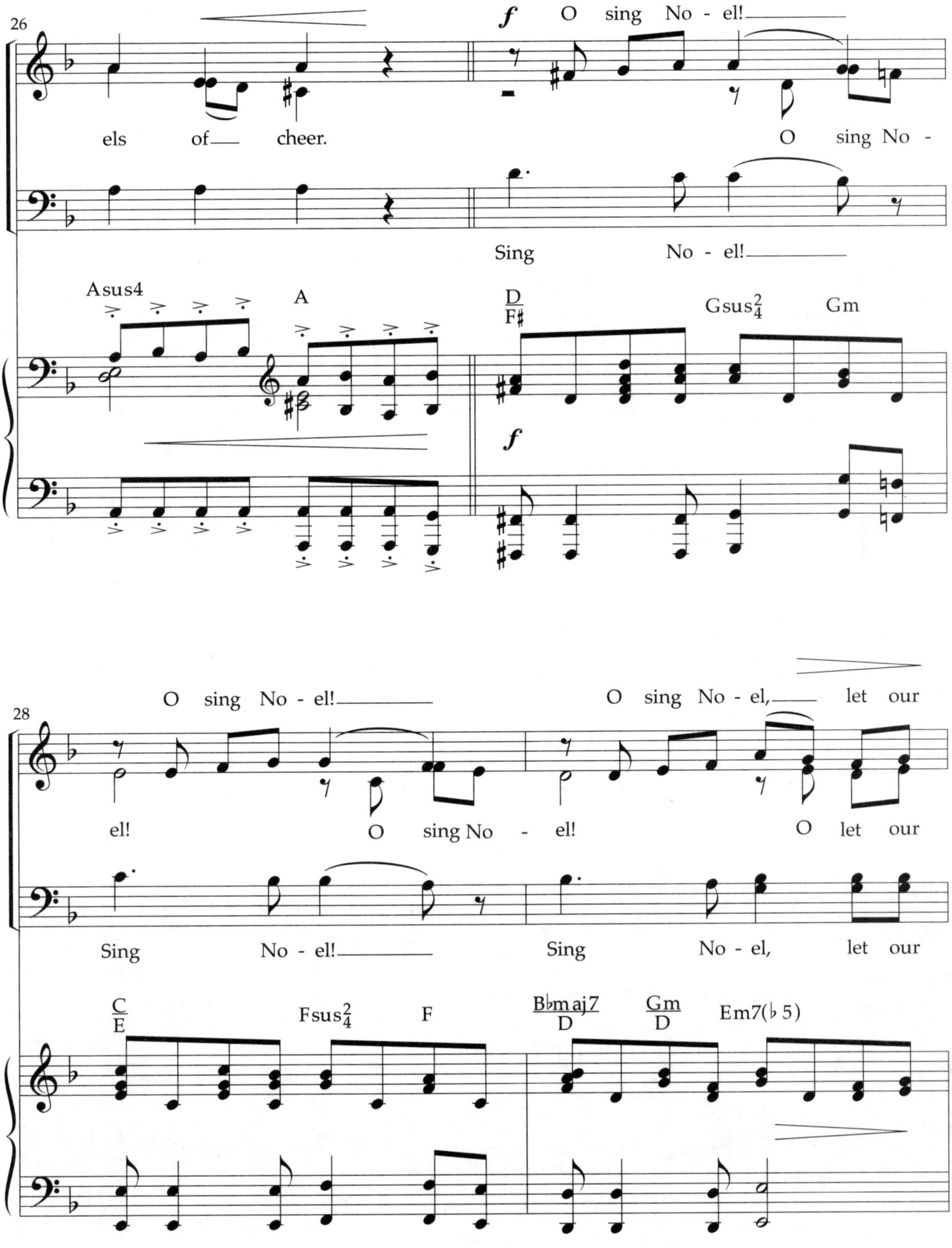
26
f O sing No - el!
els of cheer.
O sing No -
Sing No - el!
Asus4
A
D/F♯
Gsus2/4
Gm
f
28
O sing No - el!
O sing No - el, let our
el!
O sing No - el!
O let our
Sing No - el!
Sing No - el, let our
C/E
Fsus2/4
F
B♭maj7/D
Gm/D
Em7(♭5)

Still, Still, Still

DENNIS and NAN ALLEN

Austrian Carol
Arranged by Dan Goeller

Moderate Ethnic Groove (♩ = 80)

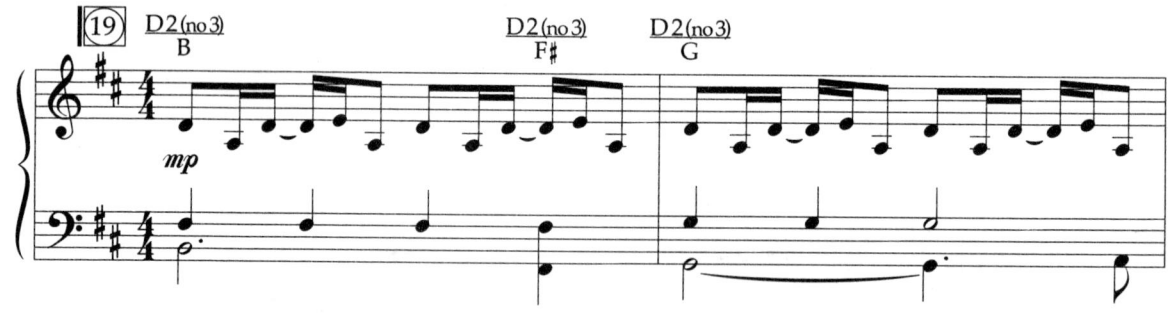

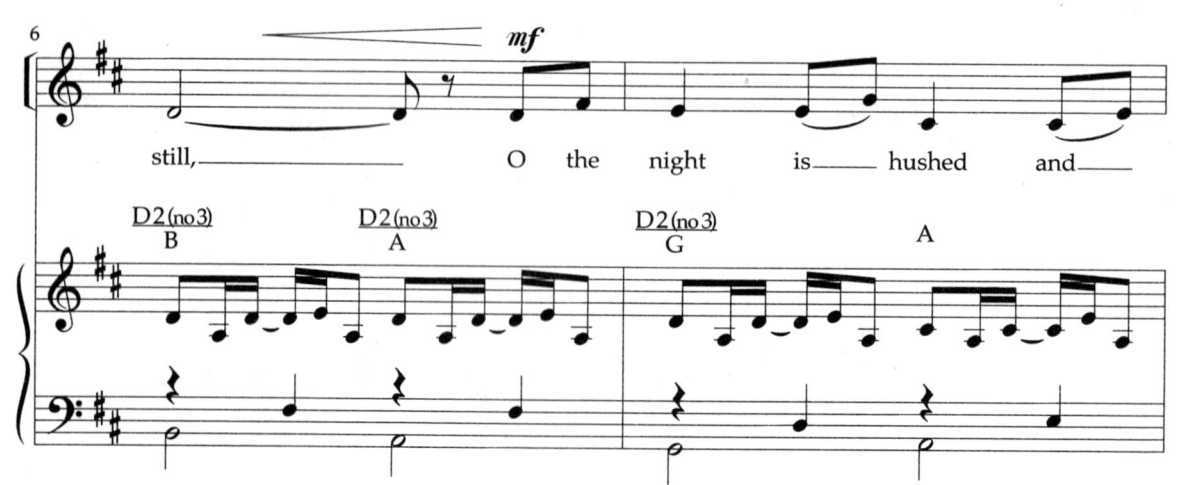

Ba - by — sleeps in — peace.

42

Still, _____ still, _____ still. _____

gradually fade

Good Christian Men, Rejoice

with Joy to the World! The Lord Is Come

Traditional German Carol*
Arranged by Dan Goeller

48

*"Joy to the World! The Lord Is Come." Words by ISAAC WATTS. Msuic by GEORGE FREDERICK HÄNDEL.

52

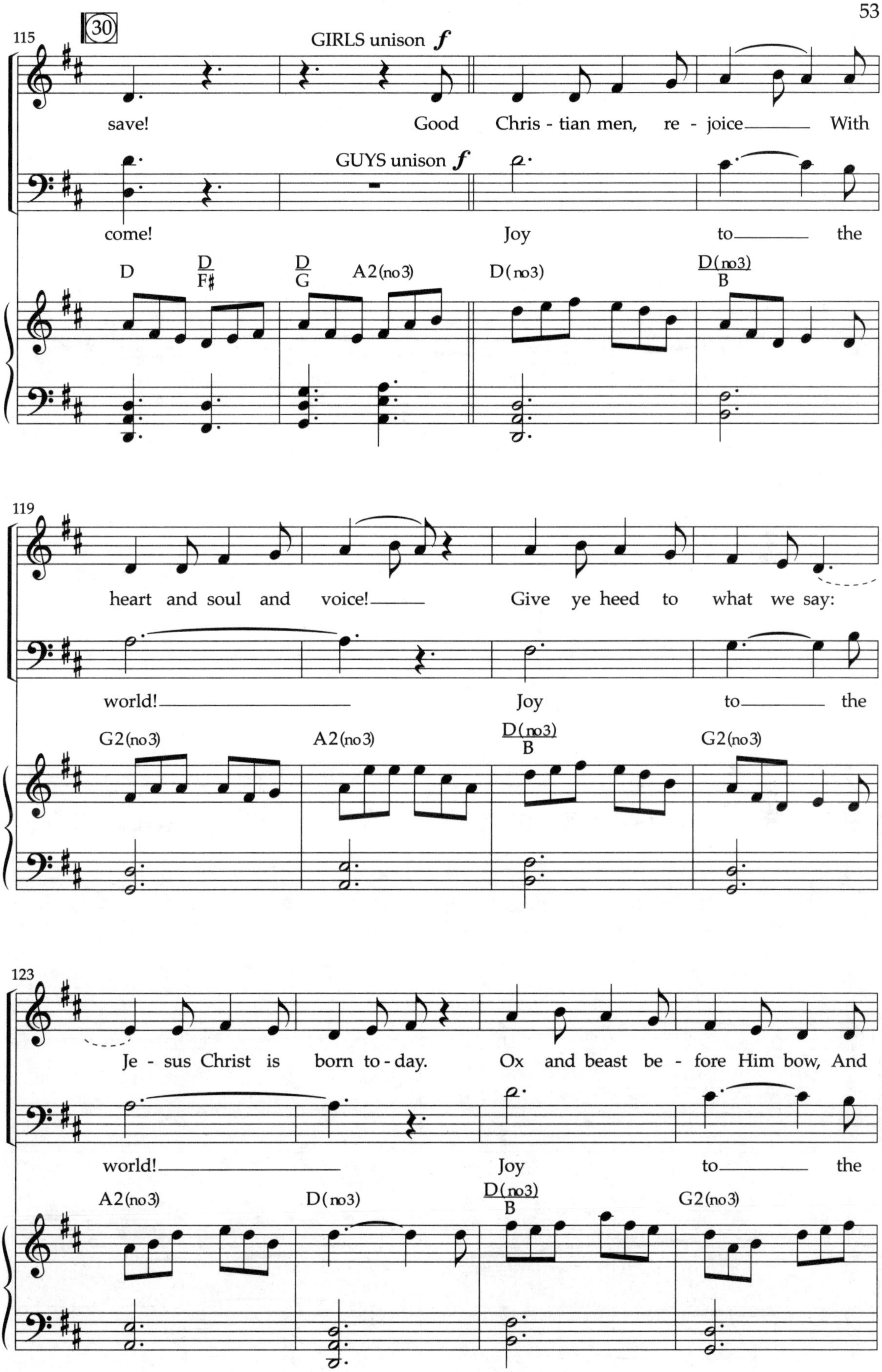
115
30
GIRLS unison f
save! Good Chris - tian men, re - joice With
GUYS unison f
come! Joy to the
D D/F# D/G A2(no3) D(no3) D(no3)/B
119
heart and soul and voice! Give ye heed to what we say:
world! Joy to the
G2(no3) A2(no3) D(no3)/B G2(no3)
123
Je - sus Christ is born to - day. Ox and beast be - fore Him bow, And
world! Joy to the
A2(no3) D(no3) D(no3)/B G2(no3)

The World's Desire
(A Christmas Carol)

G. K. CHESTERTON

DAVID HUNTSINGER
Arranged by Dan Goeller

was the world, But here is all a - right.— But
was the world, But— here is all a - right.— But
was— the world, But here is all a - right. But

here is— all a - right. 2. The Christ child lay— in Ma - ry's
here is all a - right. 2. The Christ child lay in— Ma - ry's—
here is all a - right. 2. The Christ child lay— in Ma - ry's

arms, His hair— was— like a— star.———— O

arms, His hair was— like a shin - ing star. O

arms, His hair was like— a star.——— O

stern and cun - ning are the kings, But here the true hearts

stern and cun - ning are the kings, But— here the true hearts

stern and cun - ning— are the kings, But here the true hearts

are.——— But here the true hearts—— are. 3. The

are.——— But here the true hearts are.

are. But here the true hearts are.

Christ child lay on Ma - ry's heart,——————— His

3. The Christ child lay on—— Ma - ry's heart,———— His——

3. The Christ child lay on—— Ma - ry's heart, His

What Child Is This

WILLIAM C. DIX

Traditional English Melody, 16th Century
Arranged by Dan Goeller

65

King of___ kings sal - va - tion brings; Let lov - ing hearts___ en -

throne___ Him. This, this___ is Christ, the King, Whom

shep - herds guard___ and an - gels sing: Haste, haste___ to

Sing We Now of Christmas

with Antiphonal Noel

Traditional French Carol
Arranged by Dan Goeller

Sing we now of Christ-mas, No-el,—sing we here!

Hear our grate-ful prais-es to the—Babe so dear.

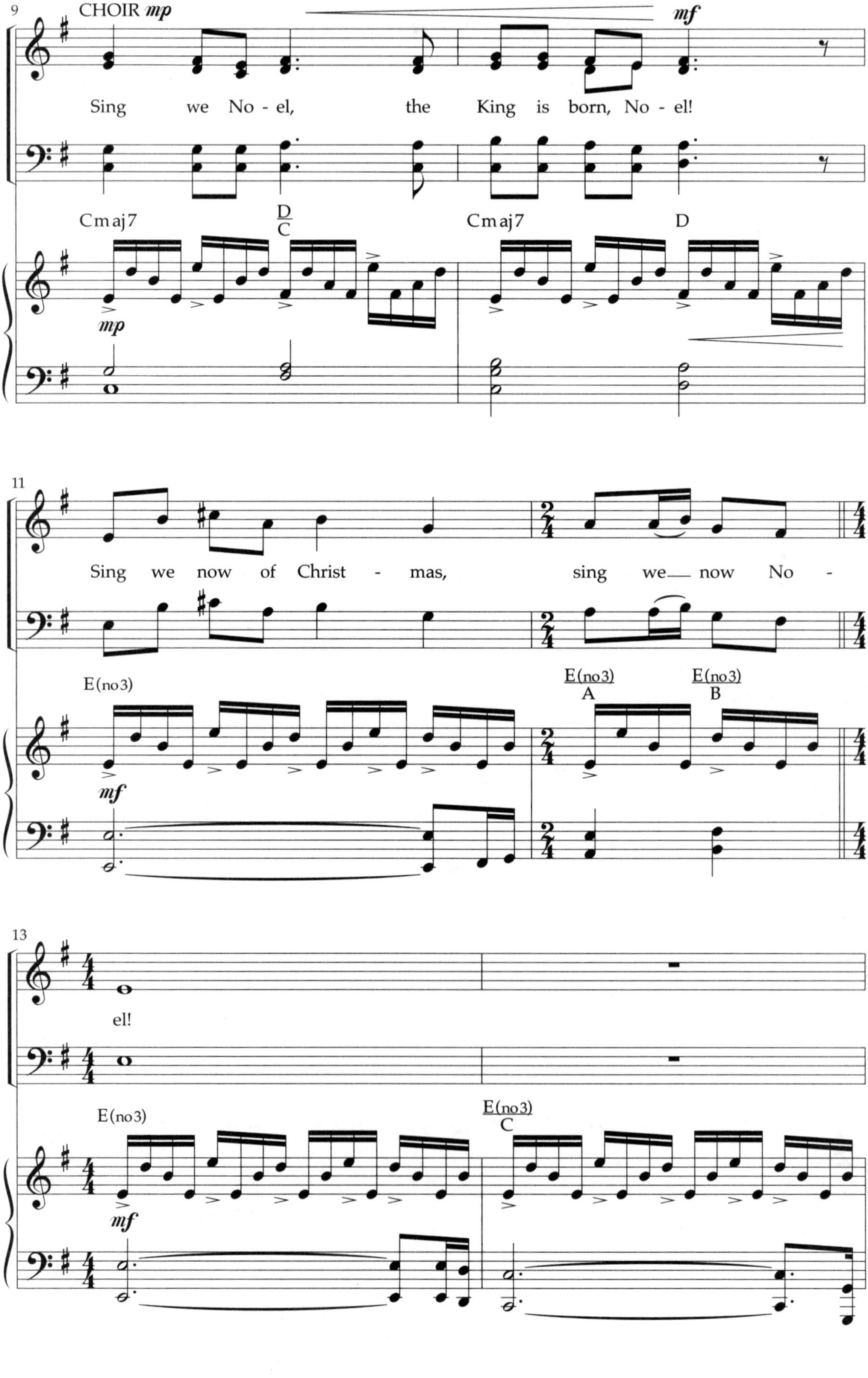
9
CHOIR mp
mf
Sing we No - el, the King is born, No - el!
Cmaj7
D
C
Cmaj7
D
mp
11
Sing we now of Christ - mas, sing we now No -
E(no3)
E(no3)
A
E(no3)
B
mf
13
el!
E(no3)
E(no3)
C
mf

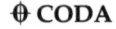

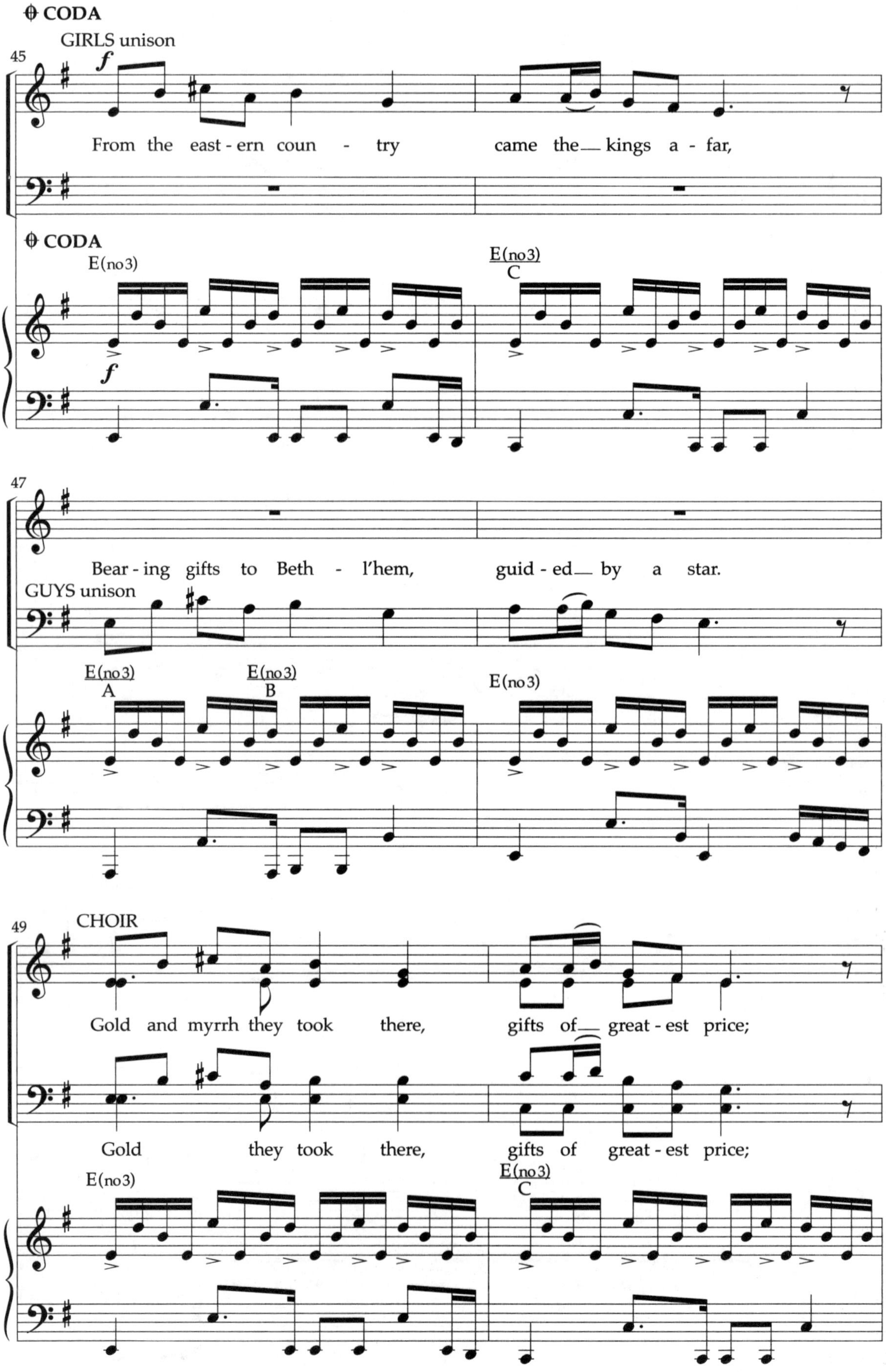
CODA
GIRLS unison
45
f
From the east - ern coun - try came the kings a - far,
CODA
E(no3)
E(no3)/C
f
47
Bear - ing gifts to Beth - l'hem, guid - ed by a star.
GUYS unison
E(no3)/A
E(no3)/B
E(no3)
49
CHOIR
Gold and myrrh they took there, gifts of great - est price;
Gold they took there, gifts of great - est price;
E(no3)
E(no3)/C

Lovely Child, Holy Child

DAVID N. JOHNSON

Traditional Appalachian Folk Melody
Arranged by Dan Goeller

*(Guy or Girl)

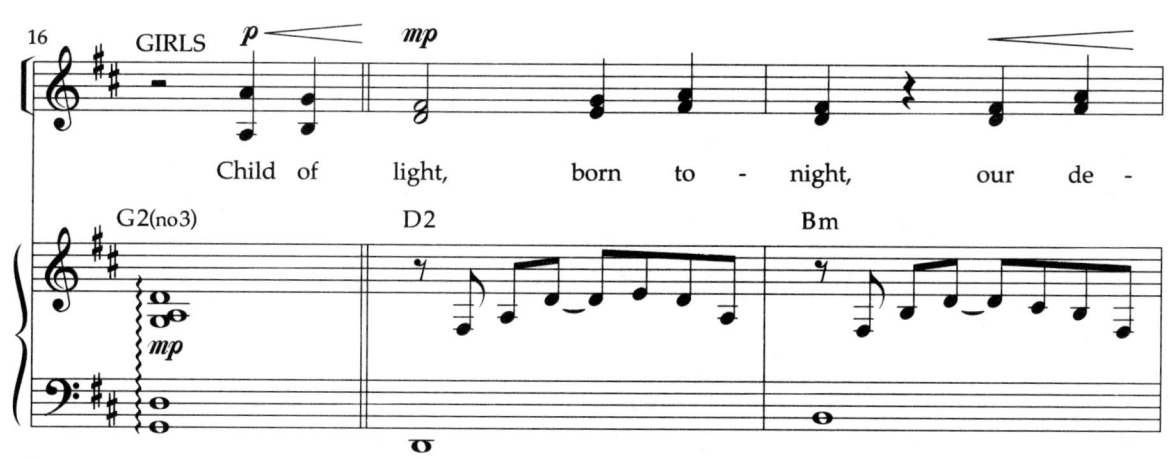

Lyrics:
ia. ___ Al - le - lu - ia, ___ al - le - lu - ia. Love - ly Child, ho - ly Child.

Chords:
Bm9 Bm D/F# Am Gsus4 G D A/C# Bm G/B
Gmaj9 Asus4 A D Am D/F#
G C/E F Bm7(b5)/D E D/F# E/G#

molto rit.

71

dored, may this word now be out - poured:

F♯m   G2(no3)   Asus4   A   Bm

molto rit.

74

mp CHOIR unison   *ten.*   *ten.*   *a tempo*

Al - le - lu - ia to the Lord.

Bm/A   G2(no3)   A2(no3)   Gmaj7/B

mp   *a tempo*

77

rit.

A2/C♯   Gmaj7/B   G2(no3)

rit.   *mp*

O Come, All Ye Faithful

Latin Hymn ascribed to John Francis Wade

JOHN FRANCIS WADE
Arranged by Dan Goeller

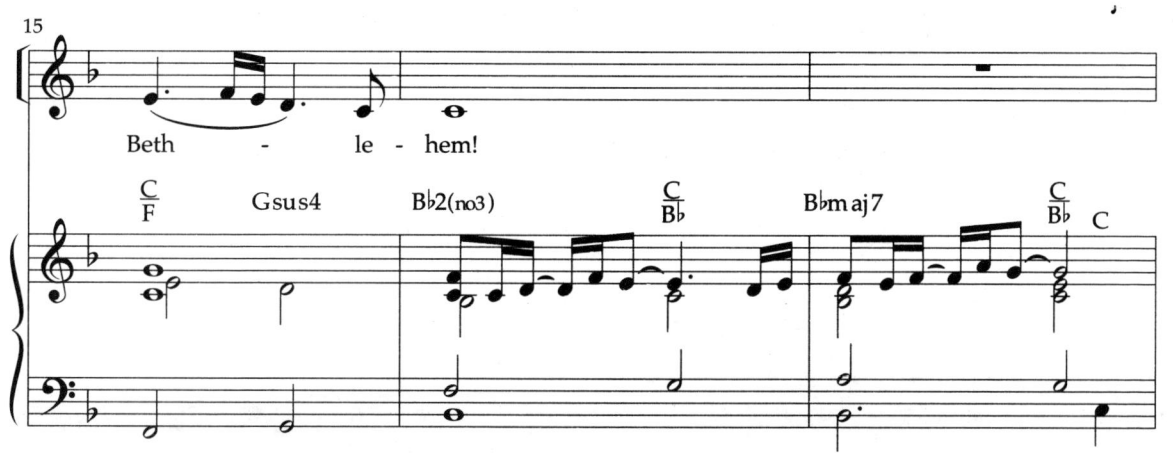

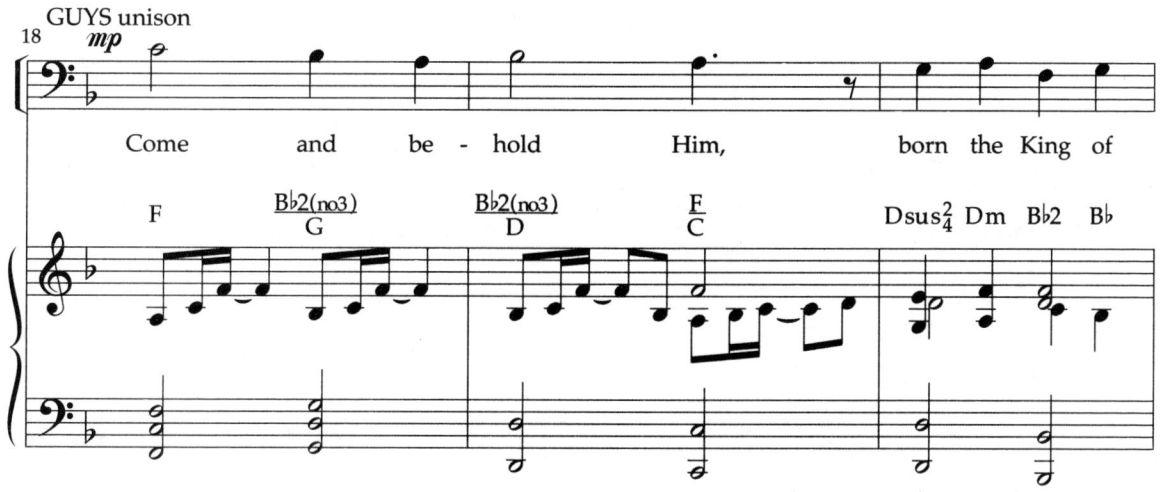

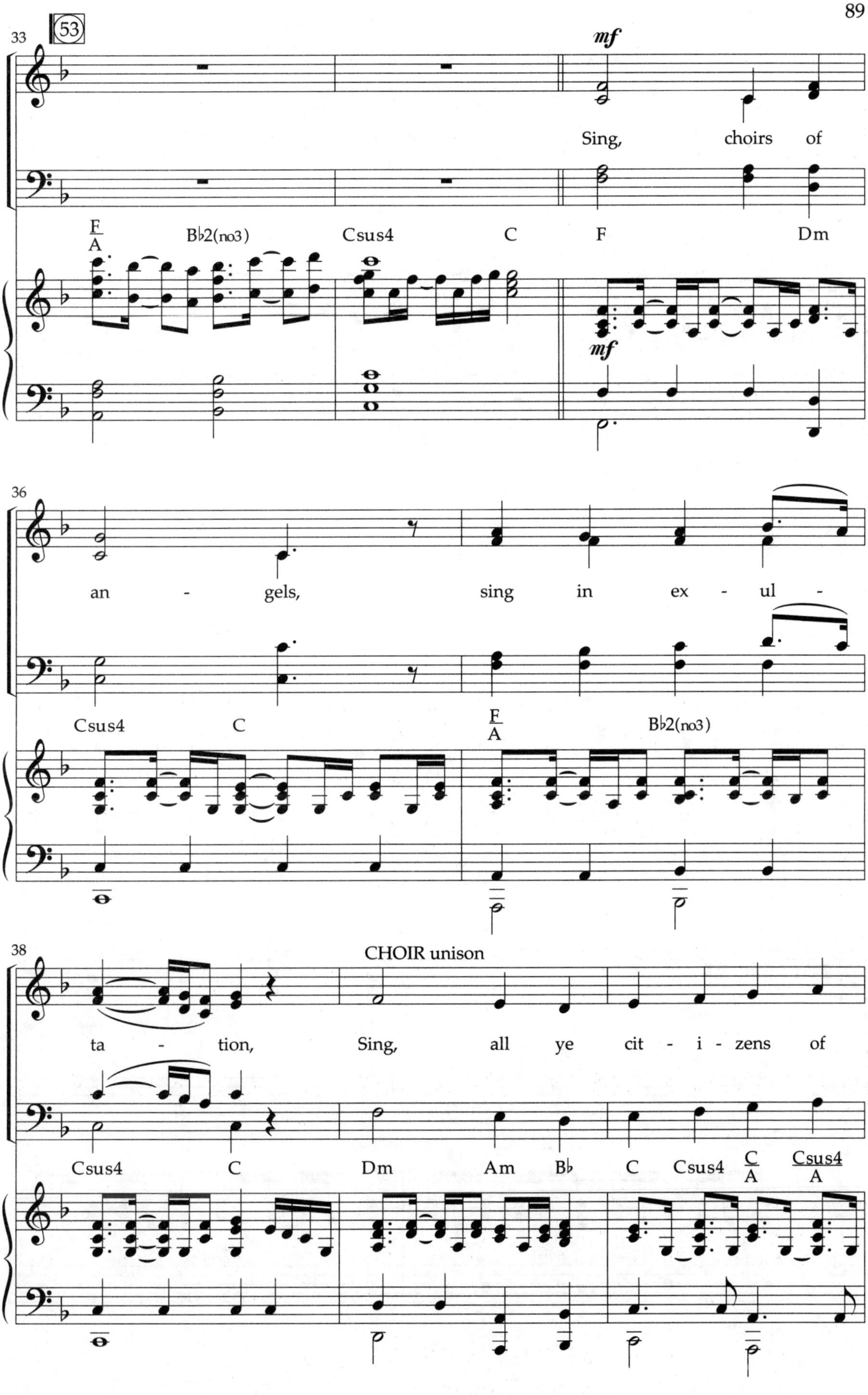
33
53
mf
Sing, choirs of
F/A
B♭2(no3)
Csus4
C
F
Dm
mf
36
an - gels,
sing in ex - ul -
Csus4
C
F/A
B♭2(no3)
38
CHOIR unison
ta - tion,
Sing, all ye cit - i - zens of
Csus4
C
Dm
Am
B♭
C
Csus4
C/A
Csus4/A

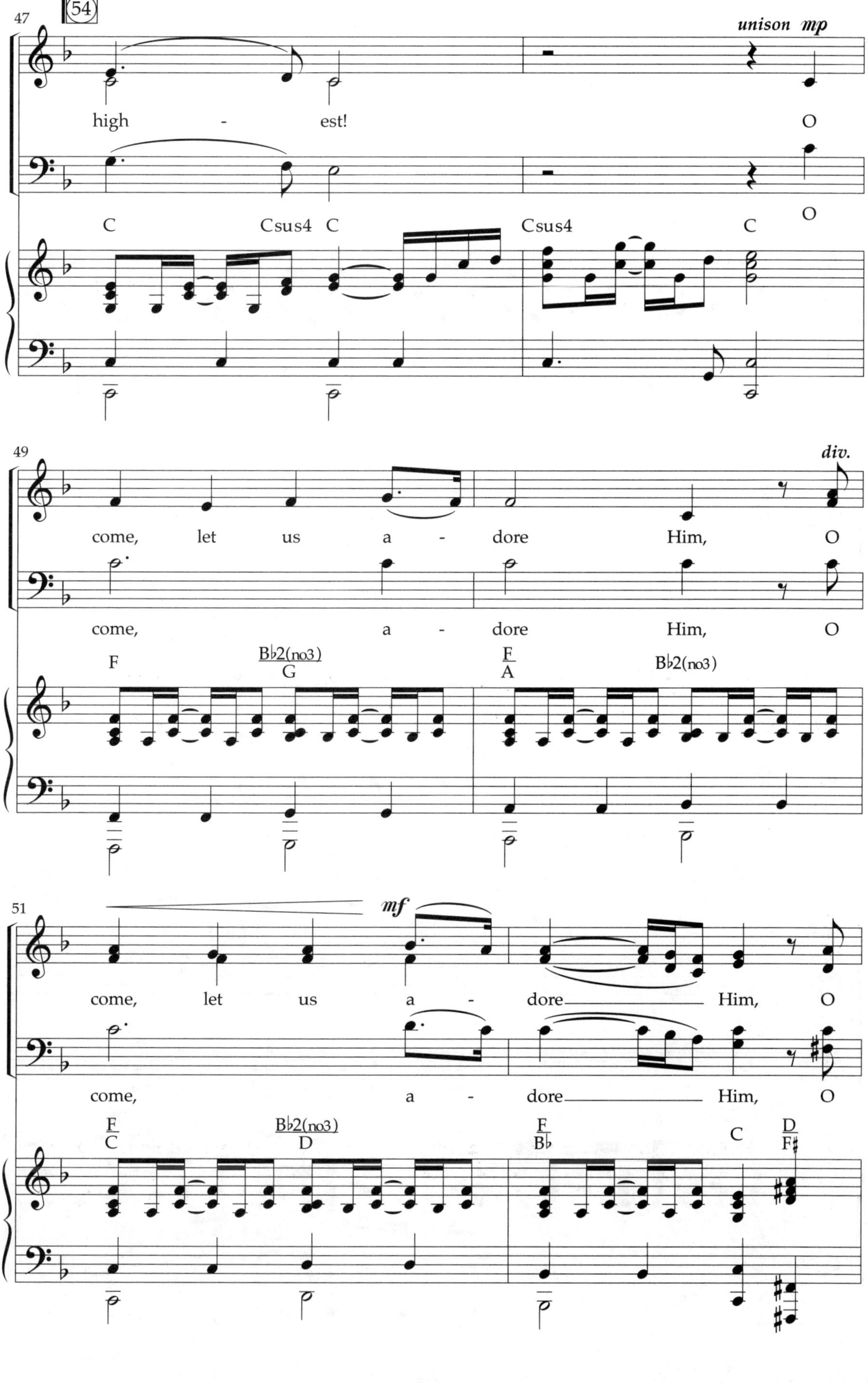
54
47
unison mp
high - est!
O
O
C
Csus4
C
Csus4
C
49
div.
come, let us a - dore Him, O
come, a - dore Him, O
F
B♭2(no3)/G
F/A
B♭2(no3)
51
mf
come, let us a - dore Him, O
come, a - dore Him, O
F/C
B♭2(no3)/D
F/B♭
C
D/F♯

What Can I Give Him?

CHRISTINA S. ROSSETTI

DAVID and BONNIE HUNTSINGER
Arranged by Dan Goeller

*(Guy or Girl)

Bring a Torch, Jeanette, Isabella!

with Angels We Have Heard on High

Traditional Provençal Carol
Arranged by Dan Goeller

Aggressive Folk Groove (♪ = 180)

CHOIR unison
mf

Bring a torch,— Jean - ette, Is - a - bel - la,

Bring a torch,— come swift - ly and run. It is Je - sus, good

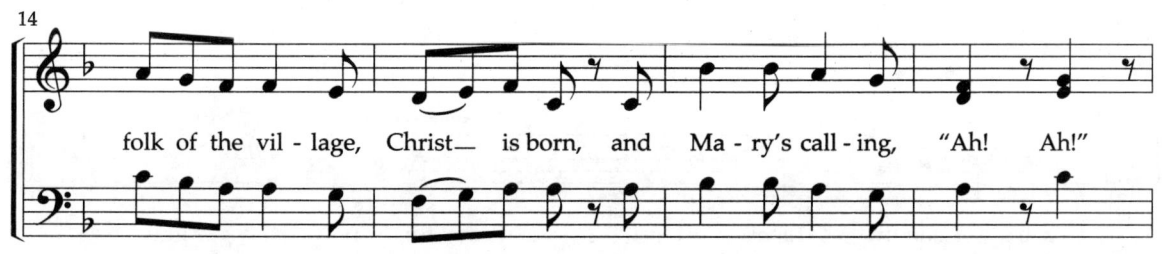

folk of the vil - lage, Christ— is born, and Ma - ry's call - ing, "Ah! Ah!"

Beau - ti - ful is the moth - er. Ah! Ah! Beau - ti - ful is her

104

73

Put on your fin - est gar - ments. Run! Run!

76

Wor - ship the new - born King.

6 CHOIR unison

81

Bring a torch,— Jean - ette, Is - a - bel - la, Bring a torch,— come

84

swift - ly and run! Has - ten now,— good folk of the vil - lage, Has - ten now,— the

88

Christ child to praise! Re - joice!

O Come, O Come, Emmanuel

Traditional*
Arranged by Dan Goeller

*Latin Hymn tr. John Mason Neale & Henry Sloan Coffin. Music Plainsong; adapt. Thomas Helmore.

Pat-a-Pan

Words and Music by
DAN and HEIDI GOELLER
Adapted from a Burgundian Carol

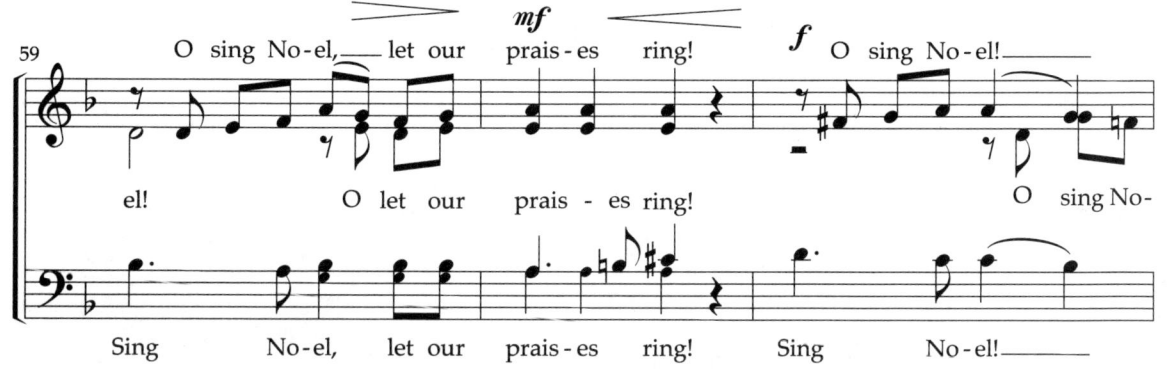

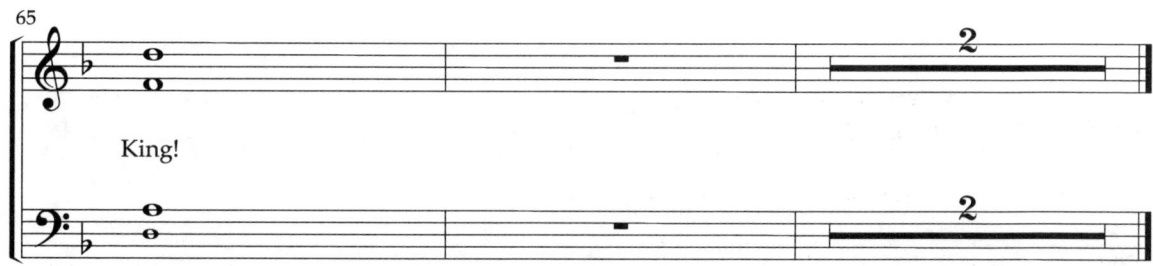

Still, Still, Still

DENNIS and NAN ALLEN

Austrian Carol
Arranged by Dan Goeller

Good Christian Men, Rejoice

with Joy to the World! The Lord Is Come

Traditional German Carol*
Arranged by Dan Goeller

122

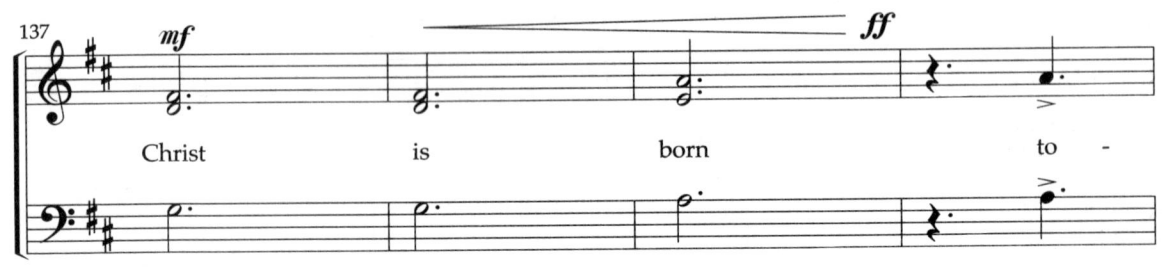

Christ is born to -

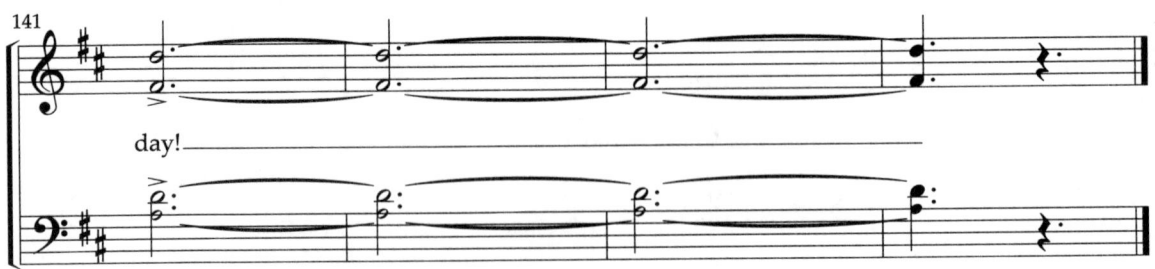

day!

What Child Is This

WILLIAM C. DIX

Traditional English Melody, 16th Century
Arranged by Dan Goeller

Babe,—— the Son,—— the Babe,—— the Son, the Babe,—— the Son—— of

Ma - ry.——

Sing We Now of Christmas

with Antiphonal Noel

Traditional French Carol
Arranged by Dan Goeller

130

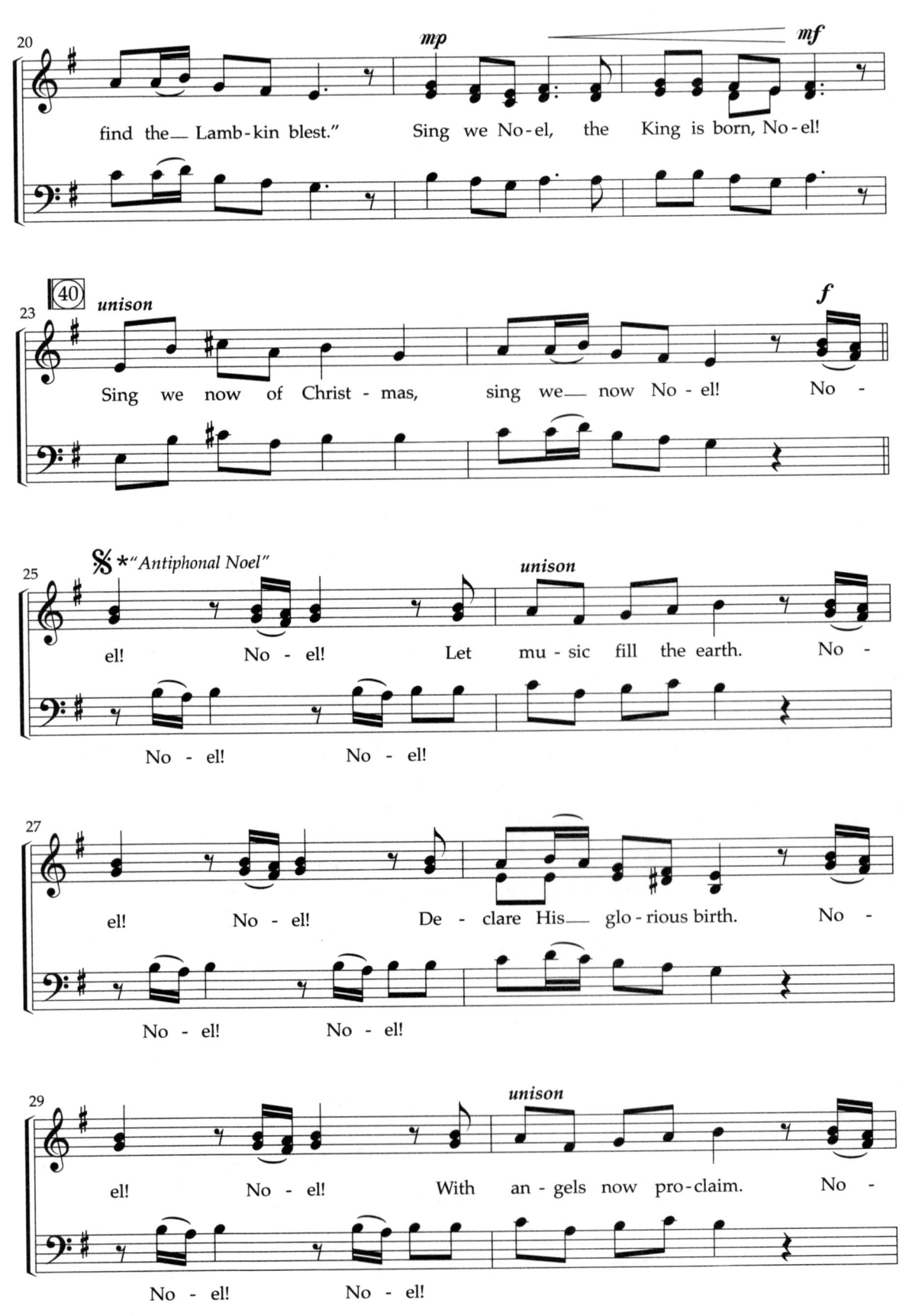

⊕ CODA

GIRLS unison
f

From the east-ern coun-try came the kings a-far,

CHOIR

Gold and myrrh they took there,

Gold   they took there,

GUYS unison

Bear-ing gifts to Beth-l'hem, guid-ed by a star.   Gold and myrrh they took there,

gifts of greatest price;   There was ne'er a sta - ble

Sing we all No - el!   Sing   No - el!

so like par-a-dise.   Sing we all No - el!   No - el!

Sing we all No-el!

Sing we now of Christ-mas,   sing we all No-el!

Lovely Child, Holy Child

DAVID N. JOHNSON

Traditional Appalachian Folk Melody
Arranged by Dan Goeller

*(Guy or Girl)

ia, al - le - lu - ia. Love - ly Child,

ho - ly Child. Love - ly Child, ho - ly

Child._____ Rest Thy head, sweet - est head; gifts we'll

spread at Thy bed; Je - sus,__ Lord,__ be a - dored, may this

word now be out - poured:_____ Al - le - lu - ia to the

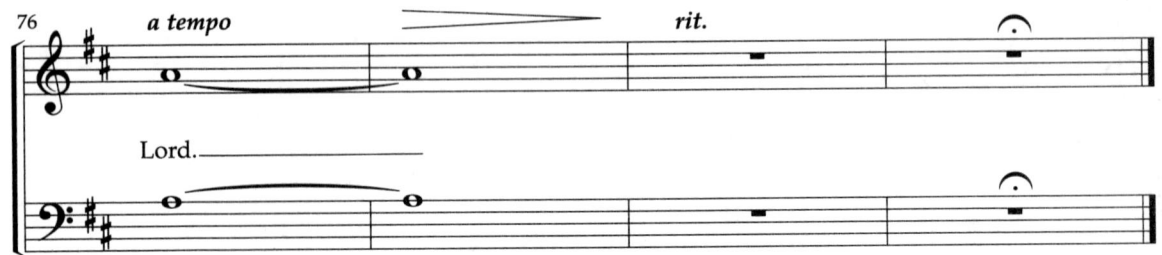

Lord.

O Come, All Ye Faithful

Latin Hymn ascribed to John Francis Wade

JOHN FRANCIS WADE
Arranged by Dan Goeller

CHOIR unison

sing in ex-ul-ta---tion, Sing, all ye cit-i-zens of

heav-en a-bove! Glo-ry to God, all

glo-ry in the high-est! O come, let us a-

O come, a-

dore Him, O come, let us a-dore Him, O come, let us a-

dore Him, O come, a-dore Him,

dore Him, Christ the Lord!

PROGRAM NOTES

Bring a Torch, Jeanette, Isabella! with Angels We Have Heard on High

Torches have always played an important role in the traditional Christmas celebrations in southern France. On Christmas Eve, villagers kept vigil by lighting torches and singing carols while visiting manger scenes constructed throughout their village. This medley captures the exuberant joy of all believers as we celebrate the coming of the Christ child. "Arise, shine, for your light has come, and the glory of the Lord rises upon you" (Isa. 60:1, NIV).

O Come, O Come, Emmanuel

The lyrics of the Advent carol, "O Come, O Come, Emmanuel," are translations of Latin verses from the Middle Ages. Originally, seven verses were used—one for each day of the last week before the Christmas celebration. In Latin, the first letter of each verse formed an acrostic. When translated, this acrostic meant, "I will be with you tomorrow." The hidden message reminded people of the Middle Ages about the promise God gave to the nation of Israel hundreds of years before Jesus was born. The prophet Isaiah wrote, "A virgin shall conceive, and bear a son, and shall call his name Immanuel" (Isa. 7:14, KJV). As we sing this haunting carol, which pleads for the coming of the Messiah, we are reminded of God's promise to all believers: "Remember, I am with you always, to the end of the age" (Matt. 28:20).

Pat-a-Pan

This traditional 14th-century French carol is attributed to Bernard de la Monnoye. The "tu-re-lu-re-lu" and "pat-a-pan" lyrics are examples of onomatopoeia, imitating the sounds of the fife and drum mentioned in the text. The imperative tone of the lyrics is reminiscent of the psalmists' declarations that we should "Shout triumphantly to the LORD...come before Him with joyful songs" (Ps. 100:1-2). "Praise Him with trumpet blast; praise Him with harp and lyre. Praise Him with tambourine and dance; praise Him with flute and strings. Praise Him with resounding cymbals;...Let everything that breathes praise the LORD" (Ps. 150:3-6).

Still, Still, Still

"Still, Still, Still" is a 19th-century Austrian carol. Its pastoral imagery and lyrical melody emphasize the hushed reverence for the Christ child lying in the manger. The final stanza alludes to the joyful celebration of heaven and earth that accompanied our Savior's birth: "Be still, and know that I am God:...I will be exalted in the earth" (Ps. 46:10, KJV).

Good Christian Men, Rejoice with Joy to the World! The Lord Is Come

"Good Christian Men, Rejoice" is an English translation of a 14th-century German carol titled, *In Dulci Jubilo.* This original form was "macaronic," which means it combined a Latin refrain, translated "in sweet shouting," with a traditional German tune and lyrics. Its lyrics are reminiscent of St. Paul's words to the Philippians: "Rejoice in the Lord always. I will say it again: Rejoice!"(Phil. 4:4). With music composed by George Frederick Handel, the famous oratorio composer, and lyrics by Isaac Watts, the prolific hymn writer, "Joy to the World! The Lord Is Come" jubilantly proclaims the joyful news of Christ's birth. We join all of heaven and nature as we "Shout for joy to the Lord" (Ps. 98:4, NIV).

The World's Desire

("A Christmas Carol")

"The World's Desire," so named in *The Oxford Book of Carols* with a different tune, was called "A Christmas Carol" in G. K. Chesterton's first collection of poetry, *Wild Knight and Other Poems.* Chesterton was a Christian writer and apologist born in England in the late 19th century. He was widely respected for his intellectual prowess and inexhaustible wit, both of which were used in numerous debates with prominent intellectuals of his day. C. S. Lewis acknowledged a large intellectual and spiritual debt to him. "The World's Desire" recounts the life story of Jesus from birth to death using similes involving the Christ child's hair and His relationship with His mother.

What Child Is This

The tune GREENSLEEVES is probably the most well-known traditional English folk song. The text for "What Child Is This" comes from William Dix's poem, "The Manger Throne." Every time we sing that question, "What Child is this?" we are reminded that many in this world still wonder about the identity of the Baby whose birthday we celebrate each December 25. We are also reminded of our opportunity to tell the good news about the living Christ, who can bring new life to all. In our modern world where we rush here and there searching for holiday gifts, perhaps we could learn a valuable lesson from the wise men who "came with haste, and found Mary, and Joseph, and the babe lying in a manger" (Luke 2:16, KJV). May we, too, make haste to bring Jesus all the praise He is due.

Sing We Now of Christmas with Antiphonal Noel

This translation/adaptation of the French carol *"Noel Nouvelet"* is one of many early noels that trace all or part of the birth narrative. Stanza by stanza, we are reminded of the various participants in the Christmas story—from Mary and Joseph to the shepherds and angels. The word "Noel" is the French word for Christmas; the English word "nowell" is a shout of joy or exclamation of delight. Just as the shepherds did, we, too, add our shouts of joy to this celebration of Christ's birth. We honor the newborn King as the wise men did who "saw the child…and falling to their knees, they worshiped Him" (Matt. 2:11).

Lovely Child, Holy Child

America has a richly diverse tradition of folk music. Negro spirituals like "Go, Tell It on the Mountain" and Appalachian carols like "I Wonder as I Wander" have become an integral part of our Christmas singing traditions. The simple Appalachian carol, "Lovely Child, Holy Child," reminds us to declare the good news of Jesus' birth everywhere.

O Come, All Ye Faithful

"O Come, All Ye Faithful" is a translation/adaptation of the 18th-century Latin hymn, "Adeste Fideles." It is one of the most popular Christmas hymns, translated into over one hundred languages. The refrain, "O come, let us adore Him," has been used separately as a contemporary worship chorus. This hymn is striking in the simplicity of its lyrics and tune. In the simplicity and humility of shepherds, we come bringing a simple song of heartfelt adoration as instructed in the Psalms: "Sing unto the Lord…and give thanks" (Ps. 30:4, KJV).

What Can I Give Him?

The text for "What Can I Give Him?" comes from the last stanza of Christina Rossetti's poem, "In the Bleak Midwinter." Rossetti was a poet during the 19th-century Victorian period in England. As we ponder the question "What can we possibly give the Creator of the universe?" we are reminded that, more than anything else, Jesus simply wants us to give Him our hearts. "With the heart one believes, resulting in righteousness, and with the mouth one confesses, resulting in salvation" (Rom. 10:10).